Grow Your Own

Strawberries

Helen Lanz

SEA-TO-SEA
Mankato Collingwood London

This edition first published in 2012 by
Sea-to-Sea Publications
Distributed by Black Rabbit Books
P.O. Box 3263, Mankato, Minnesota 56002

Copyright © Sea-to-Sea Publications 2012

Printed in China

9 8 7 6 5 4 3 2

Published by arrangement with the
Watts Publishing Group Ltd, London.

Library of Congress Cataloging-in-Publication Data
Lanz, Helen.
 Strawberries / by Helen Lanz.
    p. cm. -- (Grow your own)
 Includes index.
 ISBN 978-1-59771-313-9 (library binding)
 1. Strawberries--Juvenile literature. 2. Strawberries--Planting--Juvenile literature. I. Title.
 SB385.L36 2012
 634'.75--dc22
                        2011001221
Series editor: Sarah Peutrill
Art director: Jonathan Hair
Design: Jane Hawkins
Photography: Victoria Coombs/Ecoscene (unless otherwise credited)

Credits: Ricardo A Alves/Shutterstock: front cover t. R Carner/Shutterstock: 12b.
Chepko Danil/istockphoto: 17b. Digital Skillet/istockphoto: front cover bc, 22br.
Kim Gunkel/istockphoto: 6b. Ideeone/istockphoto: front cover b.
Magdalena Kucova/istockphoto: 6t. Robyn Mackenzie/istockphoto: 27b.
Nikonov/Shutterstock: 7c. Penny Oakley: title page, 13b, 22bl, 23b.
Achim Prill/istockphoto: 21bl. Ravenestling/istockphoto: 8br. Dale Robins
/istockphoto: 21r. Kim Pin Tan/Shutterstock: 10t. Arnaud Weisser/istockphoto: 7b.
Every attempt has been made to clear copyright. Should there be any inadvertent
omission please apply to the publisher for rectification.

Thanks to Jasmine Clarke and Tony Field for kindly sharing their gardening knowledge.

February 2011
RD/6000006415/001

To William and the one thing of all we grew that you would eat

Safety Notice:

Gardening is fun! There are a few basic rules you should always follow, however. Always garden with an adult; any pesticides and fertilizers should be handled by adults only and applied to specified plants only; wear appropriate clothing and footwear, and always wash your hands when you have finished in the garden.

Contents

Words in **bold** are in the glossary on page 29.

Why Grow Your Own Strawberries?

When you think of summer, what do you think of? Sunny days, playing on the beach, eating ice cream? What about eating strawberries? In summertime, there is so much lovely fruit to eat, including blueberries, raspberries, and delicious, sweet strawberries.

Freshness and Flavor

How about growing your own strawberries? Homegrown strawberries often have a lot more flavor and you can't beat them for freshness.

◀ Strawberries are easy to grow at home.

You Don't Need a Yard!

You don't need a lot of space to grow your own strawberries. They are happy to grow in pots and containers.

Better all Around

It's fun to grow your own, and you can be outside a lot and get some exercise. But it's not just good for us, it's also good for our **environment**, too. If we only have to step into the backyard or go to a windowsill to get our fresh fruit and vegetables, we don't use gas to drive to the store to buy them.

▲ A healthy strawberry plant will have shiny, dark green leaves.

Leaf

Crown

Flower

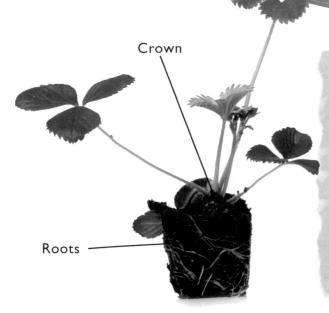

Roots

SCIENCE SPOT

Close-up of a Strawberry Plant

The roots of a strawberry plant grow from the **crown**. This is why it is important to plant them carefully, making sure the crown is just above the soil, but not too **exposed**.

Be Prepared!

So, you've decided to grow some strawberries! Before you get going, it's a good idea to prepare what you will need:

All About You...

You will be outside a lot, so you will need some old clothes that your grown-up helper doesn't mind if you get dirty. Don't forget about your feet—rubber boots or old sneakers will do.

◀ Gardening gloves, a trowel, and small fork may be useful, but not essential.

▶ You will need a watering can (or you could use a jug).

... and Your Strawberries

You can grow strawberries in most types of large container.

If you grow them in a pot instead of growing them in a plot, you will need some soil. It is a good idea to add potting mix to a pot or plot.

▲ Your strawberry plants will look attractive peeking out through the holes.

◄ You will, of course, need to buy young strawberry plants!

► It is important to feed your plants to help them to produce fruit.

Strawberry food

Top Tip!

Keep a growing diary. Write everything down, such as the type of strawberry you planted and when you did things. This will help if you decide to do it again, and will be fun to look back on. If you have a camera, you could take pictures as well.

Plants or Seeds?

You might be surprised to learn that it is usual to grow strawberries from a plant, rather than from seed.

Top Tip!

Leave buying your strawberry plants until you are ready to plant them outside. It is best to plant them out right away.

◄ You can buy strawberry plants from your local garden center.

▲ Strawberries are unusual because their seeds are on the outside of the fruit.

SCIENCE SPOT Seeds

Seeds contain all the ingredients needed to grow into adult plants. A seed can wait until the **conditions** are right for it to **germinate**, or start to grow. It usually needs to be dark, damp, and wet.

Growing From Seed

You can try growing strawberries from seed, but it can be tricky. If you do give it a try, you will have to wait for a year to see any fruit.

Before the growing season (see page 28), thinly sprinkle the seeds over damp soil in seed pots or a tray. Place in a sunny, warm spot on a windowsill. When seedlings are 4 inches (10 cm) tall, **transplant** them into bigger pots.

As the weather grows warmer, get the young plants used to being outside (see panel), before planting them out in pots or 10 inches (25 cm) apart in the ground. The plants should fruit the year after you plant them.

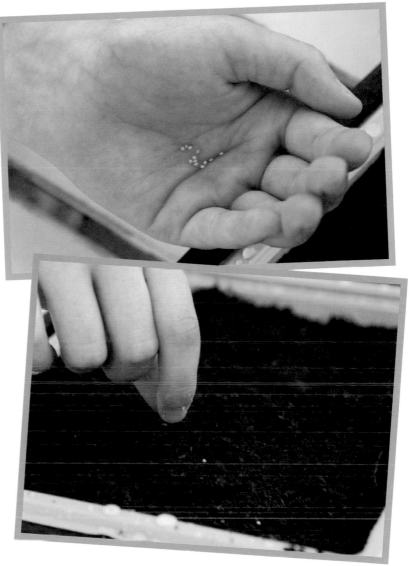

▲ Follow the seed packet instructions when sowing your seeds.

Hardening Off

If you have grown your seedlings yourself inside, it is a good idea to get them used to being outside before you plant them out. To do this, place the seedling pots outside during the day, bringing them in at night. Do this for a couple of days. This is called "hardening off."

Pot or Plot?

Strawberries love a warm, sunny spot, with plenty of direct sunlight and no shade. They do like to be sheltered from the wind.

They don't need much room and can grow in a plot or in a pot.

Preparing a Plot

Strawberries like well-prepared soil, so dig it well and add lots of manure or **compost**. As you prepare the bed, remove any weeds.

Preparing a Pot

You can grow strawberries in the specially shaped strawberry pots that have cup-shaped holes for each strawberry plant. However, they grow just as well in normal, large plant pots.

▲ *Make sure you have dug the soil well before planting.*

▶ *Specialist strawberry pots look attractive, but your plants will grow in any container.*

Put broken pottery or large stones into the bottom of your pot to help with **drainage**. Then add potting mix until the pot is almost full. If your pots aren't too big and heavy, move them around so your plants are always in the sun.

▶Broken pieces of pot help with drainage.

▲ The strawberries will cascade down both pots as they grow.

A Strawberry Cascade

You can create your own **cascading** strawberry "fountain"! Be sure to position your pots before you fill them. Use a very large plant pot on the bottom, add broken pottery pieces for drainage, and fill with potting mix. Place a smaller pot on top, toward the back of the large pot, leaving enough room to plant strawberry plants at the front of the large pot. Fill the top pot as normal.

Planting Out

▲ *For smaller pots, plant just one strawberry plant. Bigger pots will take more plants.*

Did you know that there are many different **varieties** of strawberry (see page 26)? If you choose a summer-fruiting variety, you should get fruit about two months after planting.

Planting Out

Plant out your new strawberry plants on the day you get them (as long as it's the right time of year to plant out—see page 28). Check the plant label for details of your chosen variety.

(see page 26); see page 28

SCIENCE SPOT

What It Takes To Grow

Your strawberry plant will need sunlight, water, and **nutrients** to grow. Although soil isn't always necessary for a plant to grow, it does hold the nutrients and water that a plant needs and gives the plant support to stay upright. A plant's leaves do something amazing—they use sunlight, water, and the gas **carbon dioxide** to make a store of energy to help the plant to grow.

Step-by-Step

1. Take the young plants out of their pots and soak their root balls in water for about an hour.

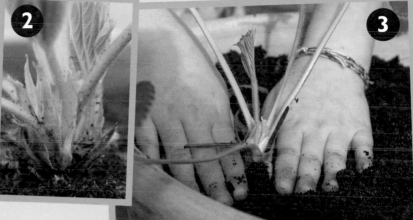

2. Dig a hole in your soil and place your strawberry plant in it. Make sure the crown of the plant (see page 7) is just above the soil line.

3. Gently, but firmly, press the soil around the base of the plant.

4. For a plot, space the young plants about 14–16 inches (35–40 cm) apart. If you have more than one row, make sure your rows are 35 inches (90 cm) apart.

5. For a pot, place one strawberry plant per cup or hole, or two plants per normal (large) pot.

6. Now all that's needed is a well-deserved drink—don't forget to give your plants one, too!

Tending the Crop

Strawberry plants have **shallow** roots. This makes them good to grow in pots, but also means you need to water them regularly, especially in hot weather. However, be careful not to overwater your plants because they don't like soggy roots!

▲ Poke your fingers into the soil to check that it's damp underneath. If the soil sticks to your fingers, the plant does not need more water yet.

Helping the Roots

Take off the first flowers to make sure the plant focuses on growing strong. This helps to get a good root system.

When the plants have become strong, ask your grownup helper to start adding a liquid **fertilizer**.

▲ Only remove the early flowers. It is the flowers that eventually form the fruits.

◄ Ask your grown-up helper to add the fertilizer to your plants' water once a week.

Runners

Your plants may produce "**runners**" a month or so after planting. Take these off so they don't take energy away from your plant in producing fruit.

▶ A runner is a shoot that comes from the main plant and develops into a new plant (see also page 25).

Runner

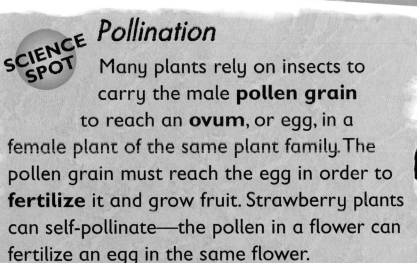

SCIENCE SPOT *Pollination*

Many plants rely on insects to carry the male **pollen grain** to reach an **ovum**, or egg, in a female plant of the same plant family. The pollen grain must reach the egg in order to **fertilize** it and grow fruit. Strawberry plants can self-pollinate—the pollen in a flower can fertilize an egg in the same flower.

▶ It is not necessary for a bee to pollinate a strawberry plant, but a bee traveling from plant to plant does make sure the flowers are pollinated evenly and the strawberries are fully formed.

Take Good Care

To keep your plants healthy you need to weed between them. This helps to protect your plants and fruit from **disease**.

Good Watering

Keep checking that the soil does not dry out. Make sure you water at the crown of the plant and try not to wet any fruit—it may make them rot.

▶ *Try to water at the crown of the plant.*

Top Tip!

It helps to cover the soil with straw when strawberries are planted in beds. Do this just before, or as fruit starts to appear. This stops the fruit from lying on the ground and getting diseases or rotting.

The First Fruit!

Keep checking your plants—you will soon see some tiny green strawberries appear. Soon the green strawberries will grow and ripen in the sun and turn into red jewels!

▶ *Water, plant food, and sunshine help the fruits to grow plump and ripen to red.*

Stop the Birds!

Be careful! The garden birds are watching, too! You will need to keep birds off your ripening crop. Putting **mesh** over your plants is one way to keep the strawberries safe.

◀ *You could also use old CDs that glint when they catch the sun to scare birds away.*

Pests and Diseases!

Sometimes **pests** and diseases can cause problems. The best way to avoid them is by checking your crop often. This way, you will notice if there are any problems and stop them before they get too bad.

▲ Clear away rotten leaves and weeds from around the bottom of your plants. This helps to prevent diseases.

Frost

Cold and **frosts** can damage your strawberry plant's flowers. If a flower has opened and goes brown in the middle because of the frost, it is unlikely it will fruit. Protect your plant by covering it with straw or scrunched up newspaper.

▲ If your fruit is going bad, check if you need to put down straw; if you are splashing the fruit when watering; or whether birds have pecked at it (pictured).

Wet

Strawberry plants don't like to get too wet. Fruit will rot if it is left to rest on soil.

Aphids

Hungry **aphids** can destroy your plants. One way to get rid of these pests is to gently brush them off with a soft paintbrush or old toothbrush. Do this as soon as you see them and keep it up until they don't return. You can also try gently washing them off with used dishwater.

Some aphids carry diseases as well. If this happens, get rid of the infected plant so it doesn't affect your other ones.

▶ *Aphids cling to plant stems and suck the sap, or juice, from the plant. This photo shows them much bigger than in real life.*

▲ *Keep a lookout for slugs! They can be yellow, brown, or black.*

Slugs

Slugs like to eat strawberries as much as the birds do. Try to discourage them by laying grit or broken egg shells around the base of your plants.

21

Harvest!

Are those berries looking red, ripe, and ready to eat? Yes? Well, that means they are ready to harvest.

Reaping the Rewards

Congratulations! This is the part that you've been waiting for. All your hard work is about to pay off! Now it is time to pick your own bowlful of strawberries.

▶ *Be sure to pick any ripe strawberries quickly so they don't rot on the plant.*

Delicious!

All you need to do now is wash your ripe strawberries in cold water and pull or cut off the green stalk.

SCIENCE SPOT *Power Food*
Strawberries are not only delicious, but they are very good for you. They contain lots of **vitamin** C. This helps your body repair itself and keeps you strong enough to fight off coughs and colds.

What Next?

Once you've harvested this year's crop of strawberries, don't forget about your strawberry plants. They will come back year after year.

◄ Strawberry plants will probably give you a good crop for five or six years before you need to replace them with new plants.

Overwintering

Strawberry plants are very **hardy** so are usually fine to be left outside over the winter. However, you will need to clear away the straw at the end of the growing season. Pull off any dead leaves so the plants are left uncluttered and healthy to face the winter.

◄ A sharp frost in the crown of a strawberry plant, out of season, can often help it produce a good crop of fruit the next year.

Propagating

During the growing season, a strawberry plant will produce "runners." These are baby or "daughter" plants that shoot out from the main plant. You can use these runners to grow new plants for next year.

Step-by-Step

1. Fill a pot with potting mix and allow the runner to root in this pot while still attached to the main plant.

2. After a month or so, when the runner is well established, you can separate it from the main plant and pot it properly. This is called propagating—or breeding—from another plant.

3. If your main plant throws out more than two runners, remove these. Otherwise the main plant will weaken, leading to a poor crop of strawberries.

Super Strawberries

Strawberries are delicious eaten on their own or with cream or ice cream. There are hundreds of recipes you can use them in too. There's one here, but you could search the Internet for more.

◄ There are lots of delicious recipes you can make with strawberries.

Strawberry Varieties

There are three summer-fruiting types of strawberry: early, mid, and late plants, all producing fruit from early into the middle of summer. There are also **perpetual** fruiting strawberries, which produce fruit throughout the summer and into the fall. There are many varieties within each group.

◄ Alpine strawberries are tiny and full of flavor—they are great for making jam.

Strawberry Cheesecake

Ask an adult to help you with the chopping and cooking.

Ingredients

Base
- 2½ cups (250 g) graham crackers
- ½ cup (100 g) butter, melted

Filling
- 2½ cups (600) g cream cheese
- ¾ cup (100 g) confectioner's sugar
- 1¼ cups (300 ml) heavy cream

Topping
- 3 tablespoons (25 g) confectioner's sugar
- 2¾ cups (400 g) fresh strawberries, hulled and sliced

Method

1. To make the base: place the graham crackers in a plastic food bag and crush with a rolling pin. Pour the crumbs into a bowl and add the melted butter. Stir to combine and set aside. Grease a 9 inch (23 cm) springform pan. Pour the crumb and butter mixture into the pan and press down. Place in the refrigerator for one hour.

2. To make the filling: beat the cream cheese and confectioner's sugar with an electric mixer until smooth. Add the cream and continue to beat until combined. Pour the mixture over the graham cracker base. Leave in the refrigerator overnight.

3. Topping: remove the cheesecake from the pan and place on a plate. Set the sliced strawberries on top. Sieve the remaining confectioner's sugar on top.

Be sure to tell everyone it's made with homegrown strawberries!

Gardening Calendar

Here's an "at-a-glance" guide to the growing year. Planting and growing times vary, depending on where you live, but you can follow these general guidelines.

Early Winter (Dec–Jan)
Weed around strawberry plants.

Late Winter (Jan–Feb)
Think about any new varieties to plant.

Early Spring (March–April)
If using seeds, sow them late in this period. Give established strawberry plants some liquid fertilizer. Prepare pots or plot for any new plants.

Late Spring (April–May)
Plant out early-bearing strawberry plants at the beginning of this period; place under **row covers** if still frosty. Plant out mid- and late-bearing strawberry plants toward the middle of this period.

Lift row covers on sunny days to allow pollination. Look for runners. Place straw under developing strawberries. Water plants well. Protect berries from birds.

Early Summer (June–July)
Place straw under developing strawberries; water plants well. Protect berries from birds. If propagating early runners, cut from main plant.

Early fruits ready to harvest at the beginning of this period.

Late Summer (July–Aug)
Keep plants well watered. If propagating mid and late runners, cut from the main plant.

Mid- and late-season fruits ready to harvest. Perpetual varieties ready to harvest toward end of this period.

Early Fall (Sept–Oct)
Give early, mid and late varieties a boost by cutting back and feeding with fertilizer.

Perpetual varieties ready to harvest at beginning of this period.

Late Fall (Oct–Nov)
Give perpetual varieties a boost by cutting back and feeding with fertilizer.

Gardening Glossary

aphid: a small, plant-sucking insect.

carbon dioxide: a gas that is part of the air around us.

cascading: a mass of something falling or hanging.

compost: a mixture of soil and rotting plants used to fertilize, or feed, plants to help them grow.

conditions: the situation or surroundings that affect something.

crown: the strawberry crown grows at the soil line. The leaves and buds of the small fruit begin here. The crown stores food for the plant and provides support for it.

disease: an illness.

drainage: in this case, to allow water to flow through the soil and leave the plant pot, to stop the soil from becoming too waterlogged leading to rot.

environment: the area in which something exists or lives and also the entire natural world—the skies, seas, lands, plants, and animals.

exposed: open to the air and weather.

fertilize: to make the soil better for growing plants by adding nutrients.

fertilizer: a substance such as manure or a chemical mixture used to make soil more fertile.

frost: frozen water droplets that freeze on the ground.

germinate: the process when seeds sprout and begin to grow.

hardy: able to survive under poor or extreme weather.

mesh: netting, often made from light plastic, to stop pests.

nutrients: something that gives goodness and nourishment needed for growing or being healthy.

ovum: the female part of the plant.

perpetual: never-ending.

pests: insects or animals that are destructive to a plant, such as slugs.

pollen grain: a fine powder produced in the male parts of a plant.

row cover: a plastic tunnel that protects plants from the cold.

runners: a shoot that comes from the "mother" or main plant, which can be grown into a new plant.

shallow: not deep.

transplant: to remove from one position and replant somewhere else to continue growing.

varieties: different types of the same plant family.

vitamin: a key nutrient that the body needs in small amounts to grow and stay strong.

Index

Useful Web Sites

www.kidsgardening.org/
The National Gardening Association's comprehensive web site for children is highly inspirational for all young gardeners.

http://howstuffworks.com/how-to-grow-perennials6.htm Information about growing your own strawberries.

www.kiddiegardens.com/growing_strawberries.html

A site that explores the subject of gardening with children, with specific advice about growing strawberries.

Gardening Club

Have you enjoyed growing your own? How about joining a gardening club? Your school may have one. You could grow fruit and vegetables, or perhaps make ladybug homes to help attract them to your garden. If your school doesn't have a gardening club, why not talk to your teacher about setting one up?

Note to parents and teachers: Every effort has been made by the Publishers to ensure that these web sites are suitable for children, that they are of the highest educational value, and that they contain no inappropriate or offensive material. However, because of the nature of the Internet, it is impossible to guarantee that the contents of these sites will not be altered. We strongly advise that Internet access is supervised by a responsible adult.